D11170962

W. SOMERSET MAUGHAM

Novelist, Essayist, Dramatist

By

CHARLES HANSON TOWNE
CARL VAN DOREN
MARK VAN DOREN
DOROTHEA LAWRENCE MANN
MARCUS AURELIUS GOODRICH
JOHN FARRAR

With a Note on Novel Writing by
MR. MAUGHAM

NORWOOD EDITIONS / 1977

W. SOMERSET MAUGHAM

Novelist, Essayist, Dramatist

By

CHARLES HANSON TOWNE
CARL VAN DOREN
MARK VAN DOREN
DOROTHEA LAWRENCE MANN
MARCUS AURELIUS GOODRICH
JOHN FARRAR

With a Note on Novel Writing by
MR. MAUGHAM

NEW YORK
GEORGE H. DORAN COMPANY

PRINTED IN THE UNITED STATES OF AMERICA

CONTENTS

PAGE

INTRODUCTION, by *John Farrar* 5

MR. W. SOMERSET MAUGHAM AT HOME, by *Charles Hanson Towne* 8

W. SOMERSET MAUGHAM, by *Carl Van Doren* and *Mark Van Doren* 13

SOMERSET MAUGHAM IN HIS MANTLE OF MYSTERY, by *Dorothea Lawrence Mann* . 17

AFTER TEN YEARS "OF HUMAN BONDAGE," by *Marcus Aurelius Goodrich* 37

TO A YOUNG NOVELIST, by *W. Somerset Maugham* 45

APPRECIATIONS OF HIS WORK 55

Books by W. SOMERSET MAUGHAM

Fiction

LIZA OF LAMBETH
THE MAKING OF A SAINT
ORIENTATIONS
THE HERO
MRS. CRADDOCK
THE MERRY-GO-ROUND
THE LAND OF THE BLESSED VIRGIN
THE BISHOP'S APRON
THE EXPLORER
THE MAGICIAN
OF HUMAN BONDAGE
THE MOON AND SIXPENCE
THE TREMBLING OF A LEAF
ON A CHINESE SCREEN
THE PAINTED VEIL

Plays

SCHIFFBRÜCHIG
A MAN OF HONOUR
LADY FREDERICK
JACK STRAW
MRS. DOT
THE EXPLORER
PENELOPE
SMITH
THE TENTH MAN
GRACE
LOAVES AND FISHES
THE LAND OF PROMISE
CAROLINE
LOVE IN A COTTAGE
CÆSAR'S WIFE
HOME AND BEAUTY
THE UNKNOWN
THE CIRCLE
EAST OF SUEZ

W. SOMERSET MAUGHAM: NOVELIST AND SO FORTH

MR. MAUGHAM'S greatest success in America followed on the publication of his "The Moon and Sixpence," which the popular critics praised, of which Heywood Broun said, "it is the most fascinating book I have read in a year." Before that, however, real appreciation of his stature as a novelist had greeted, "Of Human Bondage." Theodore Dreiser hailed it in *The New Republic* as one of the great books of our day. It reached a wide public then, and it has been more and more appreciated, more and more widely read. To-day, it is more actively studied and sought after, as the season when it was first published.

To me, Maugham, is essentially, the novelist. It is true, that even in his smallest sketches, the masterly sense of drama is there, but it is a drama always carefully founded on character development. It is, after all, the novelist's drama. His short stories, powerful studies such as "Mackintosh," "Red," or "Rain," are really tremendously compressed novels. Even his travel sketches and essays are often novels in little. Pick up "On a Chinese Screen" some time, with its variety of exotic and picturesque detail. Here you will find a scene that would be a perfect first act for a play, there a character about which several novels might easily be written. You will often discover, too, characters that appear in his long novels, sometimes in totally different guise, but the same, nevertheless. Take the lovely bit, "The Nun," for example, which immediately calls to mind the Mother Superior in "The Painted Veil." His sense of colorful background never deserts him, nor his eye for the unusual in people and events, and although his books are often highly dramatic, he is always the honest thinker, the honest realist.

When Mr. Maugham visited America last winter, the dramatization of his "Rain," originally called "Miss Thompson," and printed now as the last story in the "Murray Hill Library Edition" of "The Trembling of a Leaf," was playing to overflowing houses. After a trip to Mexico, he returned to London to witness its production and success. There followed the publication of "The Painted Veil," a short dramatic novel which many critics feel is as powerful as anything he has written. This season will witness his own dramatization of "The Letter," and, probably of "The Painted Veil," while Jeanne Eagels continues her country-wide tour in "Rain."

In the following pages the student of Maugham will discover many interesting side-lights on his work and character. The sources on him are not ready ones, as he is shy of publicity, and difficult to interview, although one of the friendliest of men. Dorothea Lawrence Mann's analysis of his life and work is a thorough and excellent one. Charles Hanson Towne, a life-long friend, writes with natural warmth and real understanding. Yet it is in his own, "To a Young Novelist," that we come closest to the man himself. We had asked him to create a picture of himself as a novelist for THE BOOKMAN.

"Sometime, sometime," he replied.

A year later, from some tropical clime where he was seeking rest and material, the vastly entertaining series of letters and replies arrived. Not only does this portray Maugham himself, but it has always struck me as being one of the wisest pieces of advice to the young writer or to the man who would really appreciate the writing of novels I have ever seen. I recommend that you read it first, before you turn to the critiques of others. With all the sardonic surface of Maugham's work and personality, there moves beneath, the immense and warm understanding of humankind that marks the truly great writer, the truly great novelist.

JOHN FARRAR.

October, 1925.

MR. W. SOMERSET MAUGHAM AT HOME

By Charles Hanson Towne

HE makes his home in London; but he really lives everywhere. For he feels that to know people one must meet people. No vicarious contacts for him! He is too great an artist not to realize that the novelist, if he is to carry conviction, must breathe into his phantom folk the very breath of life.

He knows the countries he has visited. He has not gone, like a Cook's tourist, and pecked at the Malay Peninsula. He has absorbed it. Therefore, when he writes of it, he does not pile on the atmosphere—it drips into the story he is telling, becomes mysteriously the very bone and fibre of it, and causes the reader to believe. And give your reader belief in you and you have given him all he needs.

Somerset Maugham started out in life to be a physician. It seems incredible now; yet the study of medicine caused him, later, to write "Liza of Lambeth"—that profound study of the London lying-in hospitals which could have been made only by one who had worked intimately in the poorer quarters of the English capital. Every phase of life interests him. He has the seeing eye, the almost clairvoyant ability to probe and find, not only beauty, but truth; yes, and ugliness and squalor. A universal author, let us call him; for every volume he issues is a surprise. What will he do next? He knows; but his publishers do not.

He keeps copious notes. He jots down every incident along the way, in his myriad journeyings to strange lands. Nothing is too small to chronicle. He told me once that he had the plots for forty stories in a certain little red-covered book. And scenarios for innumerable plays, any one of which he could begin tomorrow, if he so desired, so accurate is his conception of their being. And his next novel—it is all mapped out in his mind. Here is what he wrote to me about it, in a recent letter. Yet it will not be written for months. Would that more authors thus framed their work in their subconscious minds, saw with such clear understanding the motives and oblique paths of their stories.

". . . It is quite impossible for me to start on my new novel yet. For one reason, I want, before writing it, to visit again and take more careful notes of the various places in the Malay Archipelago in which the scene is laid. And since this will cost me a good ten thousand dollars you can imagine that I should not go unless I thought it very well worth while. . . . I have got all my work planned out for the next ten years, and it includes only two novels. In 'The Painted Veil' I went for a 'punch,' and I venture to think that I obtained it; but in my next novel I am going for something different. I want to get not a 'punch' but a 'throb.' I want to get in its pages the same sort of feeling you have when at night in the forest you hear in the distance the beating of drums and tom-toms. I have got the plot complete and I think it is an ingenious one. But that in the present case is not the most interesting thing to me. I want to work on the nerves of my readers by all the means I can, and I hope that this novel will be not only exciting but macabre and sardonic and humorous as well. Of course I am quite aware that I am trying something very difficult, but if I have the time and the circumstances are favorable, I think I can bring it off."

Maugham is an acute psychologist. No one fools him. He sees not only into life, deep down to its very core, but mysteriously around it. His processes of reasoning are those of a man who has found out things through suffering and pity. He has been called a cruel writer. So be it. He *is* cruel when he knows it is right, artistically, to be cruel. When, in "The Moon and Sixpence," he has *Strickland* turn upon the man who makes a business of kindness, and tell him that, damn it, he *enjoys* his self-immolation for his friends, he strikes at the bitter, ironic truth of existence. It is a terrible touch; it bites in; it hurts. But is it not true? Maugham knows that it is; and he causes the reader to know it, too.

In contrast, note the Mother Superior in "The Painted Veil." Here is a character so clearly drawn, and known and understood with such sympathetic eyes, that the reader weeps for her beautiful self-sacrifice. She emerges from the printed page, warm flesh and blood. She stands like a tower of strength in the cholera-ridden district of China, white, alone, aloof, bleakly glorious. And the same pen that drew the damnable little friend of *Strickland* drew her.

"Of Human Bondage" is one of the classics of our time. It will live, along with "Jean Christophe," "The Old Wives' Tale" and "The Forsyte Saga." A monumental novel. A deep, rich, penetrating book, packed with beauty. If Maugham had stopped there, he could have sung his *nunc dimittis* proudly. But he had other stories to tell, and he is still telling them.

A lady of intelligence who reads his short stories as they come out in the *Cosmopolitan* said to me not long ago: "I can't find a flaw in any of them—even in those little cameos which he moulds so deftly. Am I under a spell? What is his power? Sometimes the shorter tales are shallow as a fish-pool; and yet, when I've finished one of them, and think it over, I find there has been an ocean of meaning hidden somewhere. I wonder how he does it."

Ah! dear lady, that is what we all wonder. The truth is that Maugham is a master. Even his lightest comedies, such as "The Camel's Back," are stamped with his indubitable genius. And to one who has been privileged to see his manuscripts, it is interesting indeed to note the processes of his mind. What an author strikes out is quite as important to the student of literature as what he leaves intact. When Maugham changes a word, the reason is at once apparent. It would seem as if he were never quite through with his manuscript. But it leaves his hands as perfect as he can make it. Therein, I think, is one of the secrets of his success. He cares; he cares very definitely for what he writes. And that fondness for his work becomes sharply felt by his readers. His briefest pastels in prose are as carefully wrought as his long, profound novels.

He is one of the lights that have not failed. Indeed, his splendor has increased. His play, "Our Betters," that cynical comedy which bit into the bone, was revived in London last year, and created a second sensation. And it is a test of any artist to be revived. Yet "Willie" Maugham, as his friends affectionately call him, remains modest and serene in the face of his glowing success.

There is no more restful room in all London, I venture to say, than the great dining-room of his house in Bryanston Square. Here foregather the brains and wit of the English capital. He is a matchless host; and he is not afraid to ask the younger group of writers to his board. He said to me, in a burst of laughing confidence one night, "I am perfectly willing to step aside when I hear the footfall of a really fine playwright. Sometimes I sit in my study, and I think I hear a faint tapping on my door. 'There he is,' I say to myself, and jump up and turn the knob; but alas! no one at all is there!"

It may be a long time before another novelist-playwright of Maugham's calibre comes up the hill. In the meantime, while he—and we—wait, let us enjoy the genius we have among us.

W. SOMERSET MAUGHAM

(From "American and British Literature since 1890," The Century Co., New York)

By Carl Van Doren and Mark Van Doren

A RIVAL of both "The Old Wives' Tale" and "The Forsyte Saga" for the position of first place among twentieth-century British novels has been written by a younger man who in no other work has approached his masterpiece. William Somerset Maugham's "Of Human Bondage" was published in 1915, during the World War, and perhaps for that reason did not produce the immediate effect upon readers which it deserved to produce. But it has stolen quietly and surely into general estimation until now there are critics prepared to call it the triumph of its generation. However that may be, it is excellent evidence in support of the hypothesis that a writer will do his best work when he is drawing upon his own experience. Maugham, who incidentally is most popularly known for his numerous witty plays, has written several novels which have been ingenious in conception and skilful in execution. But they have been based upon situations invented for the purpose;

they have been significant for their art rather than for their life. "Of Human Bondage" is more than a situation; it is a life, and it is the author's life. It is perhaps the most brilliant of the many autobiographical novels which the present century has seen.

Passing notice may be given to a minor novel of Maugham's, "The Moon and Sixpence." It is his second-best book, and significantly enough it also is based upon the known life of a man—not the author in this case, but a modern French painter of genius, Paul Gauguin. Maugham's hero, Charles Strickland, happens to be an Englishman, but he pursues a career closely resembling that of the Frenchman. In middle age he suddenly abandons his business and his family for art, painting in Paris through years of cruel poverty until opportunity offers for a voyage to the South Seas, where he works on in comparative solitude until his horrible death from leprosy in a cottage whose walls he has covered with the finest, most mysterious products of his genius. The book is chiefly a study of temperament. Strickland is an inarticulate man who knows within himself exactly what he wants to do but who cannot express himself in any other medium than color and line. Outwardly he is callous to an almost fiendish degree; utterly indifferent to the claims of other people, he rides them down, snarling at those who would help him and contemptuous of those who condemn him. Inwardly he is filled with a vast desire for beauty of a sort which has never before been captured; this ideal he pursues to a more or less successful end. Maugham has employed all of his great intelligence, and not a little of his characteristic bitterness, in the account of this man dominated by a terrible purpose.

"Of Human Bondage" tells the story, with certain inevitable modifications, of the first thirty years of Maugham's life. He studied first in England and then in Germany; tried painting for a while in Paris, but gave it up; became a physician in London; and only later embraced the profession of author. His hero, Philip Carey, goes to school in England and Germany, spends futile years among the artists of Paris, returns to London for a medical training, and leaves the reader at the close to continue happily in a country practice. The greatness of the book, however, consists in two qualities which are independent of the plot. One of these is completeness in the picturization of life; the other is integrity in the presentation of a personality. Philip has a multitude of adventures, some of them fortunate but most of them wretched. The triumph of Maugham is that he has been able to render any aspect of existence which his hero has touched both interesting and important. The reader looks through Philip's intelligent and remarkably clear eyes at an English school, a German university, a colony of artistic failures in France, a dreary business house in London, the streets of London, a medical college, a hospital, and a village on the British coast. All these places, and many more, come as close to the reader as they did to Philip, and Maugham may digress as long as he likes in analysis or description; the words are fascinating because they are true. The gallery of characters is equally long and good; Philip's uncle and aunt, Miss Wilkinson, Weeks the American in Germany, Hayward the esthete, Cronshaw and Lawson the artists, Fanny Price the pathetic suicide, Mildred, the Athelnys, and Dr. South—these suffer, rejoice, and live forever. Philip himself, the personality through which the rich experience of the book is passed, learns much from the world, and teaches the reader much. The book is an intensely personal one. Philip is not in the least concerned, as one of Wells's heroes might have been, with showing the world how to live; he struggles to wrest from the world the secret of its own ways. Physically handicapped by a club-foot, he is inordinately sensitive to cruelty and disappointment; he is forced to ask time and again what life means, for there seems to be no reason in its behavior toward him. His conclusion is that life has no meaning which can be set forth in a formula; it is this for one person and that for another, but if one has lived thoroughly one's memories will shape themselves into a pattern as rich though as unsymmetrical as those patterns formed by the colors in an oriental rug. It is a wise young man who has learned this at thirty; a generous, intelligent, clear-minded, imaginative, and in no respect morbid human being.

SOMERSET MAUGHAM IN HIS MANTLE OF MYSTERY

(From *The Boston Evening Transcript*)

BY DOROTHEA LAWRENCE MANN

THAT clever young Englishman, Philip Guedalla, has pointed out that it is very appropriate for the United States to send a publisher as ambassador to Great Britain, since most of America's ideas concerning the English are derived from the increasing flock of English authors who come to the United States winter after winter to lecture. There is some truth in this observation, we must admit. The English novelists are rather better known at first hand by Americans than are their own novelists.

One of these English novelists, however—and he is one of the most successful and probably one of the greatest of them all—has not been seen by the American public and cannot be discussed at first hand though he has paid several long visits to the United States. He is William Somerset Maugham, author of a long list of entertaining drawing-room comedies, of the short story on which that sharp, bitter play "Rain" is founded, of "The Moon and Sixpence," the novel of the South Seas and the revolutionary genius which roused a gust of fresh interest in the French artist, Paul Gauguin, and most of all, author of the autobiographical novel—"Of Human Bondage"—one of the finest books our age can hope to produce. We know the work of Somerset Maugham in its many guises, but when the winnowing hand of time shall have had its way with the work of all this generation, I believe it will be found at last that men and women have come to understand what a truly great book was written in "Of Human Bondage."

It is by no means by the desire of Americans that Somerset Maugham passes among us so quietly. At the very time when "The Moon and Sixpence" was the novel of the hour, Mr. Maugham landed in New York, journeyed across the continent and sailed for China, without seeing a reporter! He must make an exact science of this avoiding of publicity—for he succeeds in it! His portrait is well enough known—though as usual it gives only a small hint of the man himself. It is a rather striking portrait—or rather they all are—for Mr. Maugham photographs exceedingly well. Having read his books and seen his pictures, we feel instinctively that, in meeting Maugham, we meet not only a mental giant but also a physical giant. We are so prone to discover autobiography in fiction, that we find ourselves wondering how any but the most rugged could pass successfully through his varied experiences! He has the skin of a man who has traveled much and who has been exposed to all kinds of weather. He has been an inveterate traveller all his days. He is not tall, and he gives the impression of being a rather small man, certainly no suggestion at all of the physical giant. It is, however, difficult to secure more than an external impression of him. He is singularly reticent—a man who makes his exquisite manners a shield between himself and the world. I get the impression that this may be deliberate, that he may intend to leave negative rather than positive impressions behind him. Clearly he cares nothing for the personal popularity which some authors value so highly. Mr. Maugham lived in New York last winter while "Rain" was at the height of its staggering popularity, and playing to large audiences week after week. He worked—presumably—and in the late afternoon a few privileged friends and acquaintances would come in for talk and for afternoon tea. Some of these were English, and a few were Americans.

Mr. Maugham was not destined by his family for a writing career. Nor does it appear that he was wilful or obstinate in his desire to follow his own inclinations. He was educated in medicine. He attended King's School, Canterbury, went from there to Heidelberg University, and then studied medicine at St. Thomas's Hospital in London, finally taking the degrees of M. R. C. S. and L. R. C. P., but he never practised. The fact that he took degrees in medicine has led now and again to the rumor that he was a practising surgeon, who had achieved as great distinction in that as in the writing profession. There has never been other foundation for these rumors than the fact that his family wished him to study medicine and that he acceded to their wishes in so far as taking his degree. St. Thomas's Hospital is on the edge of Lambeth, one of the slums of London which many people consider far worse than Limehouse and its attendant sections. To the hospital naturally came all sorts of cases from Lambeth, and the young doctor—whose own desires had always pointed toward writing—found a wealth of material at hand in the life of this London slum. To those people—and alas they do exist—who are prone to suggest that "The Moon and Sixpence" and "Of Human Bondage" are accidents in the career of a man who was first of all a writer of amusing drawing-room comedies, we can only say, "Read 'Liza of Lambeth'!" This was Somerset Maugham's first novel, as stark a piece of realism as we are likely to find anywhere even in our generation, which exalts realistic writing. Eliza, her mother, Jim, Thomas, all the characters of the story, drifted into St. Thomas's Hospital and fired the imagination of the young man studying to be a doctor. The book was a financial failure on its first publication in London. Nor was this a strange fate for it. It evoked no special enthusiasm in the United States where it was brought out a few years ago when Somerset Maugham was already a successful author. It is not a pleasant story in whatever way you look at it, and when it was first published it shocked Englishmen who claimed that the author had gone out of his way to libel London slum conditions.

The difficulty which surrounds "Liza of Lambeth" will always be that it lies far outside the experience of the reading public. The people who might find it natural and true of life are not the people who read books. Incidentally in the nineties, when it was first published, the public was not so well prepared for such a book as we are now. Victorian England was still in the close background, and when poverty, brutality and horror appeared in Victorian fiction they were usually sentimentalized. Mr. Maugham did not sentimentalize in "Liza." He drew a picture of Lambeth as though it were the most natural thing in the world that Lambeth should be like that. Always Mr. Maugham has had the habit of asking disconcerting questions, unanswerable questions. So he shocked Englishmen with his portrayal of the naked horror of Lambeth. It is at least two or three years since I have read "Liza of Lambeth," but I can still recall the shock I felt over the fight of Liza and the other woman in the street—women fighting as baldly and brutally as men could possibly fight in the streets, and the crowd interested in watching, but never dreaming of rescuing Liza from the punishment meted out to her by the bigger, stronger woman. To me that fight was the vivid impression of the book and I doubt whether I shall ever quite forget the brutality of that scene. It shocked me more thoroughly than any of the mental brutality which plays so prominent a part in "The Moon and Sixpence." "Liza of Lambeth" has never received anything like the recognition it deserves as a fine piece of work and perhaps it never will. Maugham has written so much that some people will feel that they have read a good deal of him without including "Liza." It may be that time will have had its way with all this generation before it is generally recognized that years before the World War Somerset Maugham had written as stark and brutal realism as anything which came out of the war.

Mr. Maugham's early ambition was to write for the stage. He was always apparently amenable to reason, however, and he did not forget that it is rather easier to get a hearing for a novel than for a play. He turned to novel writing to make his living until he should have scored a stage success. He realized as well that success as a novelist might help him to obtain a hearing from theatrical managers. In 1902 he had a one-act play produced in Germany, and in 1903—still with the idea of doing something to win the attention of the managers, he wrote "A Man of Honour" for the Stage Society. Unfortunately this play actually had the effect of prejudicing managers against him, because there were no laughs in it, and for a while he was catalogued in their memories not as an unknown quantity, but as a man who wrote the sober kind of stuff which had small likelihood of making any money for them. Those of us who have watched the tremendous success of "Rain," "What Price Glory," "Desire under the Elms" and "The Hairy Ape" know that to-day it is not necessary to write comedy or create happy endings to gain success as a playwright, but Maugham's first play was written more than twenty years ago.

In this period there is no question that Somerset Maugham, like many another talented author, suffered from the fact that there was no national theater in England, no endowed institution for the fostering of real talent and not dependent on the immediate box office receipts. For himself, Somerset Maugham realized that two paths were open. He might stick to realism, have occasional productions by the Stage Society, and by slow tortuous ways gradually get his hearing or he might write what the public wanted. He seems to have had no doubt that he could give the public what they wanted, though he hoped to be able to make them want what he wanted to give. So he turned to writing popular comedies, and there was never a moment's doubt that he did it to the public taste! That is a remarkable page in the history of modern English drama on which Maugham, the struggling realist, suddenly wrote his name in flaring letters. There was only Wilde to rival him in the staggering quality of his success. It is now a fairly old story how "Lady Frederick" came to be produced when a manager was looking despairingly for a play because he must keep his theater open, and how he picked this manuscript by chance from a pile of manuscripts which had been waiting long in another manager's closet for a reading. He had very little hope of finding anything good at all—and he got, to his own immense surprise, a play which made a signal London success. Irony has always had its appeal for Mr. Maugham, and surely there was exquisite irony here!

Once the tide turned for the dramatist, it turned magnificently. His name became a synonym for success. Since the heyday of Oscar Wilde no playwright had had four successful plays running at once in the London theaters. It is very amusing to turn back to the magazines and reviews of those days. Success seemed to dog his steps. He was in danger of being a national dramatist and the London theater of becoming Maughamized! One cynical critic remarked that as Mr. Maugham had been writing for several years, he undoubtedly had a number of rejected plays up his sleeve and it would be quite safe to give over to his care all the London theaters, as he could undoubtedly furnish them all with successes! The four plays which ran at once were "Jack Straw," "Lady Frederick," "Mrs. Dot," and "The Explorer."

All this seems strange and far away to-day, just another strange page in the remarkable history of W. Somerset Maugham. It is difficult to conjecture what other surprises he may have in store for us, but at least one never expects again to find critics speaking of him in that tolerant, half-interested fashion. There are a long list of these early plays and some of them are still acted. They played their part in Maugham's life, because their success must have made possible the life which he himself desired, a life of travelling in strange, out-of-the-way parts of the world, and writing the kind of books which he wanted to write. The fact that the things which he wanted to write have become a greater success than the early work does not seem to alter Mr. Maugham's attitude. Whatever the public reception, I feel certain that he would have done this finer work of his.

The journey of Somerset Maugham which has been most vital in its importance for us was that long-ago journey to Tahiti. He was not by any means the first author to visit Tahiti. Herman Melville, Robert Louis Stevenson, Charles Warren Stoddard, and Pierre Loti all preceded him in "discovering" Tahiti. Curiously each of these writers insisted upon discovering it and treating it as though no other authors had been there before them. To each the effect of the island seems to have been so impressive that he paid no attention whatever to the works of his predecessors. Maugham coming so much later than the others, unquestionably isolates the island for "The Moon and Sixpence." One gets no impression at all from Maugham's work that Tahiti is the chief island of the Society Group, is regularly served by steamships, has tall wireless towers, and that little Papeete ranks as a Polynesian Paris!

Hector MacQuarrie describes most amusingly his effort to find out what the natives of the island remembered of Mr. Maugham, but all Mr. MacQuarrie's efforts have really served to show us is that Somerset Maugham succeeded in living his own life as quietly and unobtrusively in Tahiti as in New York. He simply hasn't time to pose as an author—and he had no time when he was staying in Papeete. Yet he was not all unnoticed. A friend sent Mr. MacQuarrie a copy of "The Moon and Sixpence," and he suppressed the book upon the island, for the very good and sufficient reason that Mr. Maugham had given so very accurate a picture of Lavina Chapman, the half-caste, prodigiously stout proprietress of the Hotel Tiare in his "Tiare Johnson," that Mr. MacQuarrie would not trust even one person with the marvelous description. Maugham had written: "Tall and extremely stout, she would have been an imposing presence if the great good nature of her face had not made it impossible for her to express anything but kindliness. Her arms were like legs of mutton, her breasts like giant cabbages; her face, broad and fleshy, gave you an impression of almost indecent nakedness and vast chin succeeded vast chin."

Such a description might be priceless in its vividness and accuracy, but Mr. MacQuarrie dared not share it with a single friend lest somehow news of it leak to Lavina, which would "send her to bed, with gloom spread over Tahiti and no cocktails."

There is no doubt whatever that Tahiti left its impression on Mr. Maugham. He was neither then nor at any other time an aimless wanderer. He was an observer, seeking to discover the secret of the spell the South Seas has for the white man, and seeking to discover what the East did to the white man. If we take the bulk of his work which is not purely English in setting, we shall find that it comes back very often indeed to this question of the effect of the East on the white man. He has always wanted to know the effect on a man of alien climates and contacts, but his has been the detached, impersonal attitude of the observer. He has let other men do the experimenting. Looking at Mr. Maugham's clear-cut English features, we can understand that it was natural for him to observe where other men experimented. There is an attitude of detachment about him even in casual conversation, but when he does comment you realize that he has made up his mind, that he has judged as well as observed. His comment is keen and to the point and sometimes a trifle ruthless.

A good part of the effort of Mr. Maugham's writing life has gone to tabulating his observations. There is something scientific in his attitude toward them. Here, there and everywhere we find him jotting down his impressions, always with a view to their bearing on these disconcerting questions which he asks. All his South Sea Island impressions, all his Chinese impressions are there for the purpose of finding their bearing on the one big question of what the East means in its effect on other Englishmen. So far the American attitude toward the problem of the white man and the East has been largely theoretical, possibly humanitarian, but to the Englishman it is a practical problem because an appreciable percentage of young Englishmen year by year find their life work in the East.

"East of Suez" is the play which embodies most clearly the result of Mr. Maugham's observations of the white man in China. Here again we are met with the realization that he is an Englishman observing. The Englishman and the American are one in their reaction to the racial problems of the East. Their relation to the native races is not one whose morality we need to consider. The Englishman is as he is. The very reasonableness with which he seems to grant his national characteristics is proof of how little in danger he is of changing them! It is not a question of whether he is right or wrong. He simply must be considered with his own characteristics if he is to be considered at all. The history of Great Britain in its relation to the people of the Far East is written in just one way, and no amount of argument will change it. The French or Dutch or German may mingle in social equality with the native races, but the ladies of British officialdom are always white. When the Englishman marries a native or a half-caste, he has to recognize that he not only loses caste socially but that he shuts himself off from advancement in his profession. The English boy who comes out to the East filled with chivalrous idealism is very likely to be severely shocked by the callousness of this attitude among older Englishmen. Sometimes, clinging to idealism and his early moral training, he scorns the advice given him, and then he finds with withering inevitability that he has transgressed an unalterable law of British human nature. It is not only when he is a British official that this holds true. In the large businesses of the East a white man with a Eurasian wife cannot hope to hold any important position.

Running through and through Mr. Maugham's work we find insistence on these conditions. It is the magnificently disdainful gesture of Charles Strickland in "The Moon and Sixpence" that he cuts himself entirely adrift from his own people by electing to live with the natives on Tahiti. If Strickland were not an Englishman, the gesture would lose much of its decisive character. Wherever Maugham shows us Englishmen in the East, he shows this problem confronting them. The more decent the Englishman, the more impossible is the mixup into which he gets himself.

Somerset Maugham, the tireless traveller, has had plenty of opportunity to observe how the mixed marriage turns out. In "The Trembling of a Leaf," his collection of Eastern stories which contains the short story, "Rain"—originally called "Miss Thompson"—we see several facets of the problem. There is the story "The Pool," a tale of Samoa and of a Scotsman who married a pretty Eurasian. Lawson finds his problem twofold. All the women who have known him before his marriage ignore him and the men are embarrassed if they chance to meet him with his wife. His house is filled with his wife's relatives who are not even half-castes. After his child—whom he had not expected to be so brown—is born, he resolves to go back to his own country. Surely at home he will be able to make a white child of his son. There is much bitter wisdom running all through Mr. Maugham's work. These long journeys to the East have taught him Eastern human nature. There is no home for those who belong to neither race. When Lawson a few months later throws up his job in Glasgow, and follows his runaway wife and child back to Samoa, he loses caste with his wife and her people. Always Maugham is insistent on the primitive character of the brown women's attachment. He is brutally cynical about it. Lawson the suppliant has no attraction for Ethel. He is on the down grade. The only moment in this harsh story of the disintegration of Lawson's character when his wife comes near caring for him is the moment when he loses his temper and beats her. A few moments later when he apologizes, when he kneels to her and supplicates her for forgiveness, she gives him a little scornful kick. This is really the final period placed on Lawson's downfall. He is now scorned by the natives as well as by his own race. This Ethel has "all the native woman's disdain for a man who abases himself before a woman."

I should like to see the time come when the well-read person would be as unwilling to admit not having read "Of Human Bondage" as he would be to admit that he had not seen the plays of Shakspeare. "Rain" is sharp and bitter, "The Moon and Sixpence" is hard and brutal, but one may read either without experiencing personal pain. I think that few persons can have read this book without reaching some place where the pain has been so poignant that they have had to put the book aside for a time. In no other way could they endure the emotional strain of it. A friend said to me recently: "I have never been able to read beyond the point where the other schoolboys persecuted Philip and hurt his clubfoot. The book hurts too much." And I, knowing how many times and how much more grievously Philip is hurt by life than he was hurt in this schoolboy scene, could only answer from my deepest conviction: "It is a great novel. No matter how much it hurts, you are missing something you cannot afford to miss."

If it hurts so to read this book, how much must it have hurt Somerset Maugham to write it! Looking at the outward Maugham with his reserve and his correctness, seemingly so much the conventional Englishman, I realized that only so could such a man meet life. The man who can wear his heart upon his sleeve has not usually very much in his heart! The man who has felt what Philip Carey feels must protect himself with a mask. The man who could write this novel—and it is spiritual autobiography—must know gall and wormwood in the cup of life. He must realize depths of sensitiveness and suffering of which many people do not even suspect the existence.

Only a few novels ever contain the wealth of material which is crowded into this book. A more niggardly author might have found stories for a lifetime of writing all compressed into it. Fanny Price's story is a perfect instance of this. We possess the whole story of this pitiable but unpleasant girl's career—easily capable of making a full length, realistic novel of an English girl without an atom of talent but with an indomitable will who starves herself to death in Paris rather than give up the idea that teaching will make an artist of her. The sentimentalist would have gloried in ugly Fanny and her quest for beauty, but Mr. Maugham has not a whit of the sentimentalist about him. He shows her as a tragic, wrongheaded human being, utterly repulsive, leading an utterly wasted life, and dying when there was no need in the world that she should die. She is a supreme example of a tendency we all have observed in the dozens of almost talentless persons who-would-be-great. The ranks of the arts are crowded with men and women who have not the slightest chance of doing anything really worth while. Some of them love art, and some love the idea of being an artist. Whether they realize it or not, Somerset Maugham is holding a mirror up to all these with a mercilessness characteristic of him. Fortunately the majority of people are born with the ability to compromise—though Fanny Price could not—and though in their homes they go on painting their futile little pictures or writing their futile little poems and stories, they love life too dearly to die for their art.

From time to time one should make the opportunity to read the whole or at least the major part of an author's work in close sequence, because this reveals as nothing else can certain tendencies of writing, certain preferences and ideas, which might escape us, if we only read his books as they are published. Mr. Maugham is no exception to this rule. If I had not recently reread his books one after another, I would not be so certain of these facts which dominate him. On one page in "Of Human Bondage" he tells the whole story of "The Moon and Sixpence." One's first thought is that this is natural enough, since the life of the arist Paul Gauguin must have already interested him before he conceived the idea of writing a story of this sort, but the fact really is that the story he outlines in this one page is precisely Charles Strickland's story as he later told it and Strickland is a combination of Cézane Vincent Van Gogh and Paul Gauguin, with just a touch of Arthur Rimbaud, the misanthropic poet. The whole ruthlessness of Strickland is hinted here: "You hear of men painting pot-boilers to keep an aged mother—well, it shows that they are excellent sons, but it's no excuse for bad work. They're only tradesmen. An artist would let his mother go to the workhouse. There's a writer I know over here who told me that his wife died in childbirth. He was in love with her and he was mad with grief, but as he sat at the bedside watching her die he found himself making mental notes of how she looked and what she said and the things he was feeling."

Somerset Maugham differs from almost all the men novelists of this period in that he is not a woman-worshipper. The English laugh at the attitude of the American toward woman, but English books are like our own in the way in which they assume the right of women to be worshipped. Some of them unquestionably are consulting the public taste—and the fact that the larger number of their readers are women, but the feeling for women which is expressed through and through English and American fiction is very fundamental. It may be an inheritance from the Age of Chivalry, and again it may be merely an inherent characteristic of the race. Clearly it is recognizable that the attitude toward women of the English and American man is very different from that of the Continental. Maugham strives to cut through all this as he cuts through everything which does not show itself able to endure his merciless investigation. Women are certainly at a disadvantage in Mr. Maugham's books. His scorn of them he expresses again and again as he reveals their parasitic tendencies. Nearly always when we find her in his work, woman is a poisonous parasite, sapping the strength of man, using him for her own ends.

Yet such is the nature of the daughters of Eve that I fear if Mr. Maugham took to lecturing to women's clubs—as so many contemporary novelists do—he would find as Strickland did—that all his vitriolic eloquence launched against women, would only have whetted their curiosity concerning him!

In his latest novel "The Painted Veil," Mr. Maugham has combined the elements which most interest him. It is the story of an Englishman in China and of a parasite wife. In general, while Maugham's novels are far bigger work than his plays, they are written with far less attention to technique. One feels that he is more fully carried away by his substance. In "Of Human Bondage" there is really no effort at all to make it a novel of plot. It is just a human story, following step by step the life of Philip Carey from the moment when his dying mother's fingers feel for the last time the difference between his club-foot and his normal foot, on through all the vicissitudes of his existence till he reaches at least a temporary harbor. "The Moon and Sixpence" concerns itself with only the vital part of Charles Strickland's life but it follows that in simple narrative form.

Undoubtedly "The Painted Veil" is the most finished piece of work of all Mr. Maugham's novels. On it he has lavished his love of detail, furnishing exact directions concerning its manufacture. It is a short novel, designed to be read at a single sitting. Mr. Maugham has taken great pains in studying the way in which the page must look to lure the reader not to put the book down till the end is reached. He planned every detail of the appearance of "The Painted Veil" with as scrupulous care as he gave to the planning of the story itself. Though it lacks the big canvas of "Of Human Bondage" he has never been so completely the master of his art as he is here in this story of an English woman who was not conquered by her contact with the east.

W. SOMERSET MAUGHAM

Every author has his gods who have vitally influenced his work. Once again Somerset Maugham reveals his individuality. He was educated to be a doctor, made his fortune as a dramatist, and achieved fame as a novelist, but when we find him waxing enthusiastic it is over a painter, and that painter El Greco. There is no novelist or playwright or poet of whom he speaks with such feeling or to whose worship he returns with such unquestioning certainty. And the painter's influence has been felt by the novelist, I am sure, for he too seeks beauty through the medium of ugliness. Like the figures of El Greco the characters of Maugham have a troubling reality even when they seem out of drawing. Maugham, too, possesses an arresting strangeness, and I think the key is to be detected in his own words which I find in "The Moon and Sixpence" and they seem to be spoken in his own person: "Why should you think that beauty, which is the most precious thing in the world, lies like a stone on the beach for the careless passer-by to pick up idly? Beauty is something wonderful and strange that the artist fashions out of the chaos of the world in the torment of his soul. And when he has made it, it is not given to all to know it. To recognize it you must repeat the adventure of the artist. It is a melody that he sings to you, and to hear it again in your own heart you want knowledge and sensitiveness and imagination."

AFTER TEN YEARS "OF HUMAN BONDAGE"

(From *the "Book Review" of The New York Times*)

BY MARCUS AURELIUS GOODRICH

DURING the last decade, the vast, passive jury, in whose hands rests the fate of all writing aspiring to a berth among the classics, have been attending in ever increasing numbers to the steady, unacclaimed arcing over the turmoil of William Somerset Maugham's "Of Human Bondage." Among New York's literary guild the quite long book, no doubt, has been forgotten. Experiment has shown that when it is possible for a moment to shunt the attention of most of that eminent crew from the uproarious business of literature to the name Maugham, the inevitable response is an exhibitionistic shout referring to a play that he did not write, or to another novel about a tired English business man who retreated to life among the blue skies and corals with a leprosy-ridden negress.

But in the less spectacular realms of those who read books merely because they like to read, or those whose culture shelters a vibrant attraction towards authentic performances in English prose, or those who are thrilled to find the universal aspects of life on a printed page, *"Of Human Bondage" has, after ten years of steadily increasing activity, risen in England almost to a place beside "The Way of All Flesh," and in the United States is on the way to becoming an uncanonical sensation.* When the book was first published in the United States, it managed to live through three anæmic editions, despite the general critical preoccupation with other matters. Then four years went by and the publishers suddenly discovered that there was a quiet, unheralded demand for more copies of "Of Human Bondage." They issued another small edition. Two years later, without a single pat on the back from the litterateurs, the supply was again exhausted. The publishers prepared another edition. In 1923 the steady demand for the novel assumed such proportions that it was introduced into a special edition of works that seem to be in permanent demand. In this last edition, which is a fixture of its publishing house, it has gone through three printings. The universities just seem to have discovered the novel, libraries report an increasing call for it, second-hand book dealers number it among the old novels that still sell easily, and the price in London of a first edition of it has multiplied itself by three in the past five years. In New York's clubs and drawing rooms and at exoteric dinner tables, one is a bit surprised to find so old a book talked of as if it had been written yesterday, surprised that any volume could have resisted for so long the gigantic flood rushing every second from the printing presses. *The explanation, perhaps, is that "Of Human Bondage" has become a classic.*

A short time after Heinemann in England and Doran in the United States simultaneously published "Of Human Bondage" in 1915, the perfunctory, unenergetic ripple that it had caused in the critical puddle had smoothed out. In England the critics evidently had felt that something was expected of them, but most of them just did not seem to be very much interested. They admitted generally that it was a realistic character study. Richard King in the *Tatler,* as was to be expected, dismissed it facetiously in a short commentary that ended with the information that "Of Human Bondage" is scarcely a story. The *Westminster Gazette* decorously passed on the word that it had "excellence"; *The Saturday Review* admitted that it was "arresting"; *The Nation,* in a flabby article, pronounced it to be an experimental attempt to follow in the steps of Compton Mackenzie; and *Punch* inquired plaintively, "Why have so many of our novelists taken to producing enormous volumes marked by a pre-Raphaelite fidelity to detail?" In the United States the case was pretty much the same. The New York *World* in four careless, little unsigned paragraphs intimated that the novel was not worth all the space it took up and complained of the title. *Harper's Weekly* printed: " 'Of Human Bondage' is a fat, comfortable volume that will hold the attention of all those who read fiction seriously." *The Dial* commented sententiously on its length and said that "the book is far from being compellingly great."

Both abroad and in the United States, however, there were some who were fired into eloquent approval of Mr. Maugham's novel. The journals in Dublin, Ireland; Los Angeles, Cal., and Chicago, Ill., the Boston *Evening Transcript* and Theodore Dreiser in the *New Republic* came out flatly with the news that a great and thrilling masterpiece had been born into the world.

When Mr. Maugham, after fashioning a monument of such stoical brilliance as "Of Human Bondage" unmolested by overmuch critical booming, went down among the critics and burst out in their midst with "The Moon and Sixpence," his fleshy, vivid gesture was not, perhaps, so much a normal literary development, as it was a comment on the middlemen who stood between him and promptly rewarded literary achievement.

After coming face to face with the universal, simple beauty and verity that rears itself symmetrically through the 648 pages of Maugham's book, one realizes that hc confronts a tremendous emotional, not merely sensual, upheaval. *He has seen life, if not defined, at least epically epitomized.*

That "Of Human Bondage" suffered tardy intellectual approval may be due to the gaudy critical methods that began to come into vogue about the time Mr. Maugham started writing. The chief impetus behind these methods seems to be, as somebody has pointed out, an intent on the part of the critic to call attention to himself rather than to the work he is criticizing. A book received the spotlight if it were capable of reflecting sensational and startling colors back upon him who directed the light. There are in Maugham's novel no color splashing areas nor purpureal periods that could be used to decorate the sort of spectacular critiques inspired, for instance, by the efforts of Messrs. Huxley, Hergesheimer and Firbank. But "Of Human Bondage" is built with pure, meagre-syllabled phrases that twist and cling thrillingly in their unsensational contexts. *It is only when the simple, almost primitive, words sum up into the whole absorbing performance that they partake of the nature of sensation.* Without once relapsing into dullness, Maugham has consistently passed by the opportunity to indulge in poster effects, so that in the end he might attain to *a vital sweep of living, effulgent, integral color.* He has succeeded. Even in those passages wherein he depicts events and situations than which there are no more spectacular in man's existence, he maintains his Homeric restraint to an extent that almost makes them seem flat when extracted from their contexts. Here is an example:

Philip felt on a sudden sick with fear. He hurried to the house in which she lived. He was astonished that she was in Paris at all. He had not seen her for months and imagined she had long since returned to England. When he arrived he asked the concierge whether she was in.

"Yes, I've not seen her go out for two days."

Philip ran up stairs and knocked at the door. There was no reply. He called her name. The door was locked, and on bending down he found the key was in the lock.

"Oh, my God, I hope she hasn't done something awful," he cried, aloud.

He ran down and told the porter that she was certainly in the room. He had had a letter from her and feared a terrible accident. He suggested breaking open the door. The porter, who had been sullen and disinclined to listen, became alarmed; he could not take the responsibility of breaking into the room; they must go for the commissaire de police. They walked together to the bureau, and then they fetched a locksmith. Philip found that Miss Price had not paid the last quarter's rent; on New Year's Day she had not given the concierge the present which old-established custom had led him to regard as a right. The four of them went up stairs, and they knocked again at the door. There was no reply. The locksmith set to work, and at last they entered the room. Philip gave a cry and instinctively covered his eyes with his hands. The wretched woman was hanging with a rope around her neck, which she had tied to a hook in the ceiling fixed by some previous tenant to hold up the curtains of the bed. She had moved her own little bed out of the way and had stood on a chair, which had been kicked away. It was lying on its side on the floor. They cut her down. The body was quite cold.

As in "The Way of All Flesh," the hero of Maugham's book emerges from the household of an English country clergyman and climbs through public school, college, violent youth and rugged London up onto the peaceful level agony of disillusionment. In this case the climber was handicapped by a badly deformed foot. "The Way of All Flesh," it has been said, is one of the most terrible indictments of parenthood that man's mind has ever produced. "Of Human Bondage" is not merely that.

The novel takes up the life of one Philip Carey when he is almost a baby in arms, living with his newly widowed mother in a middle-class section of London. In the first few pages the mother dies and leaves Philip, sensitive and club-footed, in the hands of his uncle, the Rev. William Carey, and his childless wife. When the boy is about thirteen he is sent to King's School at Tercanbury, and from there he goes to Heidelberg. After that he tries accountancy in London, then art in Paris. The last half of the novel is built about his vivid, impecunious struggle to graduate from St. Luke's Hospital in London. Through this half of the story an implacable, pale green worm, named Mildred, crawls unhealthily: a truly remarkable character.

The book has no plot in the sense that a short story has one, but it fills spendidly that function traditionally ascribed to the novel of recording *the development of a character from the moment he becomes conscious to the moment when life has finished its major operations upon him.*

Mr. Maugham was born in Paris, where his father

was a counselor at the English Embassy. When he was between the ages of 10 and 13, he was confronted with his native land for the first time on the occasion of his going to England to become a student in King's School at Canterbury. From King's he went to the University of Heidelberg, and several years later the records of St. Thomas's Hospital in London record his graduation as a physician. His literary career began when he was twenty-one with a novel called, "Liza of Lambeth." It was written some time before he had finished with his medical studies at St. Thomas's, induced, it is reported, by a sudden pressing and romantic need for money. He has since written thirteen books, numerous short stories and twenty plays, one of which was written in German and produced in Berlin.

Well-read people often have the habit of remarking that they get a great deal more satisfaction out of reading the biography of an actual man than out of reading the most skillfully written novel. There seems to be an authenticity about the biography that is lacking in the novel. One of the striking things about "Of Human Bondage" is that it does not lack this authenticity.

TO A YOUNG NOVELIST

(WRITTEN IN RESPONSE TO A REQUEST FOR AN ARTICLE ON HIS OWN METHODS OF WRITING)

BY W. SOMERSET MAUGHAM

(From *The Bookman*)

xxx, Beacon Street, Boston,
The Twenty Third of September,
Nineteen Hundred and Twenty Four.

MY DEAR MR. MAUGHAM:—

I trust that you will pardon a total stranger writing to you and will give a few minutes of your time to answering a question which I am going to put to you. I am sure that you are very busy and I would not take the liberty of asking your advice if I were not fully determined to take it. To cut a long story short my son is about to leave Harvard and has determined to adopt a literary career. His intention is to write chiefly fiction and I should be very grateful if you would tell me in a few words what you would recommend him to do now. I am anxious to do everything in my power to assist him.

Cordially yours,

FRANCES VAN BUREN HALE.

W. SOMERSET MAUGHAM

Hotel Gotham,
New York City,
Sept. 27, 1924.

MY DEAR MRS. HALE:—

Give your son one thousand dollars a year for five years and tell him to go to the devil.

Yours very faithfully,
W. S. MAUGHAM.

xxx, Beacon Street, Boston,
The Thirtieth of September,
Nineteen Hundred and Twenty Four.

MY DEAR MR. MAUGHAM:—

I am entirely at a loss to understand your answer to my letter. I do not think that my request was unreasonable and I cannot think it deserved a reply which if I hesitate to call uncivil you will not be surprised if I consider strangely flippant in a writer of your standing in the literary world. I regret that I troubled you and beg to remain

Yours truly,
FRANCES VAN BUREN HALE.

Hotel Gotham,
New York City,
Oct. 2, 1924.

MY DEAR MRS. HALE:—

I am much grieved that you were displeased with my answer. I had no wish to be impolite and I was very much in earnest; I was brief, which I thought you wished me to be, and I gave you advice which I knew to be direct and which I thought was sensible. Your son is about to leave Harvard and therefore may be presumed to possess at least the elements of a liberal education; I can imagine no better grounding for any one who desires to be a writer, and from your letter I judge that he has been brought up in easy circumstances. He will doubtless have spent most of his life among ladies and gentlemen. This is a class which from a literary standpoint rests now under a cloud and I daresay it merits the contempt of that large body of writers who do not belong to it; but after all it ventures still to exist (though judging from the plays I have lately seen in New York and the novels I have read you would hardly suspect it) and it is well for the writer to know its habits and customs. It is possible even that he may wish to write about it. I am prepared to believe that life is more significant in a delicatessen store than in an apartment on Park Avenue and that the emotions of a truck driver are more subtle than those of a person of quality; but there *are* persons of quality and there *are* apartments on Park Avenue and the writer is wise who regards nothing human as alien to him.

So far so good.

Your son, I suppose, has led a sheltered life and at his age he can hardly have much knowledge of the world. I do not know how you can better help him to acquire this than by taking the advice I gave you.

On a thousand dollars a year he cannot starve, but if he is of an adventurous disposition (and unless he is he will not desire to be a writer) he will often find himself penniless and so obliged to do whatever he can to get his dinner. That is not bad training. On this sum he can travel all over the world, but only under conditions which will throw him in contact with all sorts and kinds of men. He will not be able to afford the luxury of respectability. Besides, in telling him to go to the devil you will have explained to him that you mean him to attach the widest possible meaning to that hackneyed phrase. If he has any spirit he will soon find an infinite number of ways and means to carry out your suggestion and in five years he will have gathered experience and an acquaintance with men and women which cannot fail to be of great value to him as a writer. If at the end of this period he cannot write then you must console yourself with the reflection that he lacks what no thought of yours nor advice of mine can give him: talent.

Yours very faithfully,
W. S. MAUGHAM.

xxx, Beacon Street, Boston,
October the Fifth,
Nineteen Hundred and Twenty Four.

DEAR MR. MAUGHAM:—

I am sorry if I seemed a little abrupt but I will frankly confess that I could make neither head nor tail of your first letter. Of course I see now that you had no wish to be discourteous or flippant. But all the same I do not think I quite agree with the things you say. Surely it is not necessary for a writer to live in an extraordinary manner any more than it is necessary for a violinist to wear long hair. Miss Austen wrote her admirable novels without ever leaving the respectable circle in which she was born and Mr. Henry James whose novels I am sure you appreciate as highly as I do both in England and America never to my knowledge moved in any world but that to which he was entitled by his birth and position. It has been my privilege to know Mrs. Wharton for many years and though she has lived so long in France I can vouch from personal knowledge for the fact that she has never ceased to be a refined and accomplished gentlewoman. I cannot help thinking this proves that there is no reason why a writer with talent should not write a successful book without taking such a hazardous course as you propose for my son.

But I daresay I did not put my original question quite clearly. What I really wanted your advice about was more the technique of novel writing if you understand what I mean. This is a matter on which a young writer naturally stands in need of guidance and I can only say on my behalf as well as on my son's that I should be sincerely grateful for any hints you can give him.

Yours most cordially,

FRANCES VAN BUREN HALE.

W. SOMERSET MAUGHAM

Hotel Gotham,
New York City,
Oct. 10, 1924.

DEAR MRS. HALE:—

I am somewhat embarrassed to know how to answer your letter, since in the last seventeen years I have written but four novels and so can only look upon myself as an amateur: I am sure that there are a great many people who are much better qualified than me to give your son hints on this difficult matter. All I can usefully do is to tell you what is my own practice, and the first thing that strikes me is that I have no habitual practice; it seems to me that every novel must be written in an entirely different fashion, and so far as I am concerned each one is in a way no more than an experiment. Each subject needs a different treatment, a different attitude, and even a different manner of writing. The only rule I know which is always valid is to stick to your point like grim death. Much harm has been done to the art of fiction by the opinion widely held some years ago that the novel was a suitable vehicle for ventilating every sort of view and advocating any kind of theory. Writers who wanted to preach sermons, urge reforms, or castigate abuses threw their ideas into the form of fiction. They produced a large number of very tedious novels. I cannot help thinking that to entertain is sufficient ambition for the novelist, and it is certainly one which is hard to achieve; if he can tell a good story and create characters that are fresh and living he has done enough to make the reader grateful. I certainly find in myself no urge to reform, admonish, or instruct my fellow men, and if I desire information about town planning or the Montessori system I shall not look for it in the pages of a novel.

You will not have failed to notice that many novels are written which have every possible excellence and yet are quite unreadable. I hope you will not think it a wilful eccentricity when I tell you that I look upon readableness as the highest merit that a novel can have. They say that it is better for women to be good than to be clever; that is a point upon which I have never been able to make up my mind; but I am quite sure that it is better for a novel to be readable than to be good and clever. I have often wondered what it is exactly that gives a book this quality. I will not tell you all the conclusions I have come to but only one or two points which seem to me to tend to that admirable result.

I think first of all that the writer is wise to be brief. I like a novel which can be read at a sitting and for my part, when I am writing one, I use every device I know to persuade the reader to do this. Then I think he should pay greater attention to his form than English and American novelists—influenced by the heresy that the novel is a ragbag into which can be thrown any matter that comes along—habitually do. If so many novels nowadays did not start without a beginning and leave off without an ending it would seem absurd to point out that a good novel should have a beginning, a middle, and an end, and all its parts should be duly balanced. A novel should have an inner harmony and there is no reason why the reader should be deprived of the delight which he may obtain from a beautiful proportion. In this connection I strongly recommend your son to read Carl Van Vechten's "The Tattooed Countess." He will find in it a model of form which alone makes the book a pleasure to read; and he will find also ingenious characterization and an enchanting humor. He cannot read it attentively without obtaining from it valuable instruction, profit and edification. It is a perfect example of perhaps the most difficult book to write: the light novel.

I think the writer is well advised who writes simply. I would have him use the plainest words and put them in the most natural order. I have no patience with the writers who employ bizarre constructions and make a parade of unusual epithets; nothing goes out of fashion so quickly as affectation nor is anything so stilted as the modish phrase of the year before last. I know one eminent novelist who spends much time studying all manner of dictionaries in order to find unexpected words. I cannot imagine a more trivial occupation. I have noticed that the writers who use these odd and extraordinary words do not always know their meaning. I knew another writer, now happily dead and forgotten, who was so eager to be distinguished that he wrote "ends and odds" for "odds and ends." Let not your son be afraid of the hackneyed phrase; it may very well be the most suitable. Above all he should be clear. I do not think the writer has a right to ask the reader to puzzle over his meaning. If he knows it himself he can put it in plain terms; if he is unwilling to do this he must be very sure that it is profound enough to repay the reader's trouble when he has got to the bottom of it. Nothing is so tiresome as the obscurity which envelops a commonplace. But let not your son think that if he writes soberly, clearly, and plainly he must eschew beauty: Swift achieved an admirable style by using the simplest words and by putting them in the most natural order. It is not the resounding epithet which makes good English, but the accurate and sensitive ear.

I am afraid that these suggestions will seem unsatisfactory and haphazard to you. They are what immediately occurred to me; but of course the subject is complicated and you must not for a moment think that I imagine I have said all that there is to be said about it.

Yours very faithfully,
W. S. MAUGHAM.

xxx, Beacon Street, Boston,
The Thirteenth of October,
Nineteen Hundred and Twenty Four.

DEAR MR. MAUGHAM:—

It is very good of you to have written me such a long and careful letter, but since I wrote to you last my son has decided to go into the bond business. I do not suppose that you will leave this country without coming to Boston and when you do Mr. Hale and I will have much pleasure in making your acquaintance. I shall be At Home on the first and third Wednesdays of the month all through the winter.

Yours most cordially,

FRANCES VAN BUREN HALE.

P.S. I am surprised at your writing *than me.* Surely it should be *than I.*

The Bookman. February 1925.

APPRECIATIONS OF THE WORK OF W. SOMERSET MAUGHAM

Novels

OF HUMAN BONDAGE

The boyhood, youth and early manhood of a middle-class Englishman forms what is probably the most deeply plowing study of all Mr. Maugham's works. Philip Carey, son of a surgeon, is orphaned at nine, and is brought up in his uncle's country vicarage. From there he goes to a boys' preparatory school, where his club-foot, about which he is painfully sensitive, brings down upon him the native cruelty of the young British schoolboy; thence he proceeds to an upper school, passes through the religious experience, becomes disgusted with further school life and insists upon studying in Germany instead of going to Oxford. In Germany he sloughs his religious beliefs, but retains his Christian ethic. His fortune is a very small one, and he turns to the only profession at once gentlemanly and open to his means—chartered accountancy. He fails, studies art in Paris, fails at that, and ultimately takes up medicine. Such is the thread of the story. And its intent is given in its title. For Philip discovers that all men are bound and his own sense of freedom is a sense that may well be an illusion.

"To some it has apparently appealed as a drab, unrelieved narrative. To me at least it is a gorgeous weave, as interesting and valuable at the beginning as at the end. I found myself aching with pain when, yearning for sympathy, Philip begs the wretched Mildred, never his mistress but on his level, to no more than tolerate him. He finally humiliates himself to the extent of exclaiming, 'You don't know what it means to be a cripple!' The pathos of it plumbs the depths. The death of Fanny Price, of the sixteen-year-old mother in the slum, of Cronshaw, and the rambling agonies of old Ducroz and of Philip himself, are perfect in their appeal. Mr. Maugham has suffered for the joy of the many who are to read after him. By no willing of his own he has been compelled to take life by the hand and go down where there has been little save sorrow and degradation. The cup of gall and wormwood has obviously been lifted to his lips and to the last drop he has been compelled to drink it. Because of this, we are enabled to drink it. Because of this, we are enabled to see the rug, woven of the tortures and delights of a life. We may actually walk and talk with one whose hands and feet have been pierced with nails."—THEODORE DREISER in the *New Republic.*

W. SOMERSET MAUGHAM

THE MOON AND SIXPENCE

When that striking and terrible story, "Of Human Bondage," appeared some three or four years ago, intelligent readers at once knew that whether or not one liked his work, Somerset Maugham, the novelist, was a notable and original writer. This early impression will be deepened by his new book, "The Moon and Sixpence." Now, tales of persons declared by their creators to be geniuses are by no means uncommon; but it is very uncommon indeed for the reader not to remain entirely skeptical regarding their extraordinary gifts. And here it is that Mr. Maugham scores and scores heavily. No less clever is the leisurely way in which he builds up the atmosphere for his story, giving us, to begin with, a good idea of the sort of man through whose eyes we are to see Strickland and the outward, semi-public events of Strickland's life. He is a powerful and impressive figure, a man who fascinates even while he repels. His comments are sometimes brilliant. Mr. Maugham is always shrewd,—often disconcertingly so. He has a way of getting beneath the surface and bringing to light what he finds there, putting forth his discoveries in a style which though clever is never permitted to become merely smart. "The Moon and Sixpence" tempts to lengthy comment and frequent quotation; it is not a book for lovers of saccharine, but for those who prefer to have their fiction "mixed with brains."—*The New York Times.*

W. SOMERSET MAUGHAM

THE PAINTED VEIL

When Kitty Garstin,—beautiful, thoughtless Kitty—married her husband, it was because she couldn't bear that her younger sister should be married before her. There was no question of love involved. Then came tragedy and the slow birth of Kitty's soul in agony and exaltation. From the first explosive sentence of this book that hurls the reader into a situation tense and breathless, to Kitty's last passionate cry of hope, the absorbing interest of this drama of three lives never slackens.

"Mr. Maugham's latest book is a splendid story superbly told."—JOSEPH COLLINS in the *International Book Review*.

"He is the novelist of the inner-self, the searcher of our hearts and spirits and very souls, the revealer who looks, not always with pity but never with disdain, upon our supreme stupidities. I repeat, 'The Painted Veil' is a tremendous novel."—CHARLES HANSON TOWNE in the *New York Sun*.

LIZA OF LAMBETH

"The first book launched by Somerset Maugham, 'Liza of Lambeth,' could hardly have been, considering its slight dimensions, a clearer indication of the line he was to follow. It came out at a time when Gissing was still in favour, and the odour of mean streets was synonymous with literary honesty and courage. There is certainly no lack of either about this idyll of Elizabeth Kemp of the lissom limbs and auburn hair. The story pursues its way, and one sees the soul of a woman shining clearly through the racy dialect and frolics of the Chingford beano, the rueful futility of faithful Thomas and the engaging callousness of Liza's mother."—GRANT OVERTON, in *"When Winter Comes to Main Street."*

THE MAGICIAN

"In 'The Magician' W. Somerset Maugham has struck a new vain. It is a story in which black magic and the course of true love are intermingled and form a highly exciting narrative. The book is as striking, 'tis said, as anything the author has yet written, and that is saying much. He makes no compromises with incredulity. The demons and devils of the black world are realities; the ghastly experiments of Paracelsus, who created life and fed his creatures with the blood of virgins, are the basis of the story, which is but a daring excursion in the territory of the occult."—*Philadelphia Public Ledger.*

MRS. CRADDOCK

"It dates back almost to his beginnings as a novelist, but it is by no means the work of a prentice hand. It is a keen and powerful exposition of a marriage that within a few years ends in a miserable failure for two reasons. The first reason is a difference in temperaments, and the second results from the fact that the wife's station in life as a member of a wealthy county family is above her husband's, for he is merely a prosperous gentleman farmer. At the outset, moreover, it was really Bertha Ley's passionate obsession of love for Edward Craddock that brought them together. If the matter had been left to Craddock, there would have been no ensuing romance with its mingling of comedy and tragedy. She made up her mind that she would be his wife and she had her way. Even the vehement opposition of her guardian was unavailing."—E. F. EDGETT, in the *Boston Evening Transcript.*

"There is a sense of the fluent quality of life—the sense of the mystery of existence and human passion that an artist can only achieve in humility."—*New York Tribune.*

THE EXPLORER

"'The Moon and Sixpence' was quite a fine piece of work but 'The Explorer' needs no borrowed plumes or reflected glory to insure its own success. Considered *à l'Amèricaine,* purely as a story, the book is absorbing from start to finish. As an exhibition of the art of character drawing it is quite as remarkable."—*The New York Evening Post.*

Short Stories

THE TREMBLING OF A LEAF

Under the general title "The Trembling of a Leaf," the author of "The Moon and Sixpence" and numerous other novels of more than ordinary excellence presents a study of the effect of the South Pacific Islands on white men. The effects are unpleasant mostly, but the studies are not entirely unsympathetic. The stories are bold, colorful, dramatic, tragic. One thinks of them as real. There is gripping realism in the character drawing.

"Honolulu" is a story one will read more than once. So is "Macintosh" to mention two in the group. The delicious South Seas atmosphere envelops insidiously the yarns so cleverly spun. There is beauty, warmth, languor, and, of course, silver shores and glimmering lagoons. But bestiality and death, too. All that glitters in and about Tahiti is not gold, Mr. Maugham would have the world know. Some of the stories are queer—one expects them from this writer—some shocking, but all have charm, and they fascinate. They are vivid, real, glowing pictures, and doubtless will win a high place in the heap of current South Pacific literature.—*New York Sun.*

"The last story ('Rain') is a masterpiece, flawless. At the same time on comparison with some of the other tales, one should add that it stands only *primus inter pares.*"—*New York Post.*

A Book of Sketches

ON A CHINESE SCREEN

"Sharply etched with an artist's economy of strokes are these brief studies of the motley mêlée of humanity —French, Indian, English, Chinese, American— which varying interests have brought together in China. Mr. Maugham singles out a figure here and there and tells a tale of it, quaint or impressive, terrible, amusing, always unexpected. He brings out all its inherent drama or tragi-comedy and leaves the moral, if there is one, to the reader."

"A book of sketches, 'On a Chinese Screen,' are genuine; they are excellent . . . the sort of thing an English traveller is adept in doing."—LAURENCE STALLINGS in the *World.*

Plays

EAST OF SUEZ

"East of Suez," from the first scene, in which not a word is spoken, to the last, in which there is not a word to say, shows once more Somerset Maugham's uncanny knowledge of the effect on white men of alien climates and contacts. There have been few more powerfully dramatic plays than this in which the Occident is confronted with the mystery and exotism of the East.

THE CIRCLE

"Bright dialogue, scintillating cynicism, rare reading, even if in the end you disagree with the sentiments set down. 'The Circle' can fairly be said to represent W. Somerset Maugham at his best."—LENSHAW, in *Detroit Free Press.*

". . . comedy of manners filled with the author's characteristic wit and humor, now genial and suave, now dry and puckery with a bit of a sting. . . . One of the best.—*Providence Journal.*